SELECTED
POEMS

OF RAYMOND SOUSTER

EDITED BY MICHAEL MACKLEM

OBERON PRESS

811
5725λ

Poets commonly either are or pretend to be different from other people. They see things more clearly, they feel things more intensely. They do no recognizable work. They keep to themselves, smoke pot, make love (inexhaustibly) and write poems.

Raymond Souster isn't at all like that. Though he's recognized by most critics as one of Canada's most significant poets, he's hard to distinguish from the man on the next stool at Murray's. He wears suits, his hair is short and he works every day at the Bank of Commerce at the corner of King and Bay. He has a wife and a home in Toronto's west end, where he grew up. He has three cats. He is fifty years old.

These are the facts you have to begin with with Souster. They are central to all his poems. It's not enough to say that Souster is a square. You have to go on to say that we are all squares if you dig deep enough. Nobody is born a freak — not even bpNichol. We are all born squares. Some of us later become freaks, but even if we do we remain squares below the surface. The freak shows us things we didn't know existed. A poet like Souster does something quite different. He shows us things that are already familiar. He is himself familiar — we can see him any day on any downtown street in Toronto — or in Winnipeg or Ottawa or Hamilton or Halifax or even (though he would be less comfortable there) in Vancouver. Every poem he writes is intended to do just one job: to make us see ourselves and the everyday world we live in — just as we are, just as it is — more clearly, more honestly than ever before. We read Souster for the pleasure of *recognition*.

Souster was born in Toronto in 1921. His father, then 27, had been working since the age of fifteen for the Standard Bank of Canada. The Standard became the Commerce in 1929 and Austin Souster stayed with it for 30 more years until his retirement in 1959. His mother had been a stenographer and book-keeper.

    I can almost see

    my father's canoe
    pointing in from the lake,
    him paddling,
    mother hidden
    in a hat of fifty years ago.

The next year the Sousters moved to a house on Indian
Grove in Toronto's Humberside district, later moved into
the nearby Runnymede district. Souster went to public
schools in the area, then on to UTS and Humberside Col-
legiate. He graduated in 1939 and started work with the
old Imperial Bank, which later merged with the Com-
merce. Apart from four years in the RCAF (four crucial
years in Souster's development as a poet), he has worked
there ever since. After the war he met and married a girl
who was working in the bank — the Rosalia of the many
dedications. They moved into a house in Swansea, later
moved back to Humberside, where they still live. This
strong sense of *neighbourhood* is important to Souster.
He has spent his whole life, apart from the war years, in
one neighbourhood, in the world of the late thirties where
he grew up.

    Good to be back
    in the old house. To hear the toilet's
    sudden boil and simmer-down. To walk
    along the upstairs hall and know
    where the floor will creak and not creak:

    to find the same cobweb
    crouched in the same secret corner,
    to feel faithful bed-springs
    warm to their work again!

Think of him as living next door to the Woodleys.
    Souster began writing poems before the war, but it wasn't
until the fifties, back home in Toronto, that he developed
the style he has since made his own. (More than half of

Ray and Lia, 24 *June,* 1947

the poems in this selection were written after he won the Governor General's Award in 1964.) The poems he published during the fifties and sixties created a world as solid and tangible as the streets and houses of the Toronto he grew up in.

> Street of my boyhood
> (I lived right around the corner),
> quiet, leaf-heavy street
> of West Toronto.
>   Here,
> behind that house, in the lane,
> from garage roofs we ambushed
> the Nelles Street gang,
> pinned them down with catapults,
> then, out of acorns,
> forgot all our strategy
> and ran like hell.

One of the central symbols of this world is baseball. Souster started throwing a ball at the age of six and by the time he was thirteen had pitched himself into the City of Toronto bantam baseball championships. He later played for neighbourhood teams and still later he showed up in service leagues. After the war he played softball for various bank teams until he retired at the age of 42. For the

At home after a ball game

mature poet baseball stands for the world of his boyhood, for a time of innocence:

> Vitore, Bugala, Moszyniski, where are you now?
> Angelis, Croswell, Calgone, what has time done with you?

> You wouldn't remember me, the kid brought up
> for a taste of senior ball. But I remember
> all of you, after twenty years and more,
> just like yesterday. . . .

He remembers, but the world he remembers is gone: "like everything else/that was too good to last." He winds up pitching rotten apples, in his "best Columbus Boys' Baseball Club style," at a hole in the side of a tumbledown barn. The demolition of the old Maple Leaf Stadium is to the poet "one more little death among so many dyings":

> life will go on, still beautiful and strange, but
> never in quite the same way as yet another boy-
> hood fantasy goes under. . .it's all gone, there's
> nothing left to do now but go on home, grace-
> fully, if possible, this time without even as much

as a bright-coloured rain-check in the pocket,
which found months later in kinder days still
promised baseball in another year. . . .

Between youth and manhood, the sandlot world of the
thirties and the steel and concrete world of the present,
Souster draws the thick black line of the Hitler war. For
Souster the war was the beginning of all endings:

That was our last year of baseball: the War waited
    for us.
No more dusty hours on the diamond, the hand-
    throbbing sting of the bat
stroking line-drives, no more third strikes with a
    round-house curve.
The War waited for us, to take us, to grind us,
at the end of the season!
                        O Krycia, Wagman, McDowell,
heroes of my youth,
                    where are you now?
                                And where
    am I?

If his four years in the RCAF taught Souster anything, it
taught him that might is seldom right. Events like the
bombing of Dresden in 1945 were for him a very deep and
very personal kind of initiation.

The RAF called it
The Dresden Special. . . .

One hundred thirty thousand
charred bodies jammed together
between two bread slices.

But even at that
jolly old Sir Winston
had no trouble lifting it

> in his pudgy fingers.
>
> After a bite or two
> he smacked his lips, grunting,
> *Just the way I like Nazis,*
> *very well done. . . .*

For all his honesty, Souster is incapable of dealing real-istically with the problem of evil. Evil for him is the work of established institutions. Nature itself is innocent. It was inevitable that he should blame the Dresden bombing, not on the elements of human nature that led to the war in the first place, but on Winston Churchill and (by implication) the Air Force brass.

This attitude to evil is extremely important in all of Souster's work. It explains the peculiar importance in his poems of such figures as birds and flowers, beggars and cats (but never dogs) and above all lovers and loving. These are all emblems of Souster's Garden of Eden — a cluster of images associated with plants and animals, boyhood and youth, desire and innocence.

> It's a kind of flower
> that if you didn't know it
> you'd pass by the rest of your life
>
> But once it's pointed out
> you'll look for it always,
> even in places
> where you know it can't possibly be.
>
> You will never tire
> of bending over to examine,
> to marvel at this,
> the shyest filigree of wonder
> born among grasses.
>
> You will imagine poems

as brief, as spare,
so natural with themselves
as to take breath away.

Souster seldom writes of flowers with such delicate beauty
as this. Cats touch him more nearly. Like flowers they
stand for the good and gentle things the establishment
destroys, and the poet identifies easily with them.

A thick mucous film
now covered the eyeball.

Out it comes or she'll die
the vet warned us.

Better have her destroyed
someone else said.

Today she lives on
in our house,
number one
one-eyed cat.

No trouble at all
with the good right eye
of our love.

This is a world too of drunks and derelicts, tramps and
beggars — all signs of the indifference and inhumanity
("My battered Christ/of Yonge Street") of the city that
created and destroys them.

The love poems are among the most interesting. There
is the expected contrast between love and pleasure on the
one hand and the outside world (equals the city equals in-
difference, inhumanity) on the other. Some of these
poems seek only to convey a sense of the safety and com-
fort to be found in a familiar bed, a familiar woman.
Others convey a greater sense of wonder: "Your warm

sun circling/my earth of amazement."

> Porcelain-white
> smooth jug
> of your body
>
> slowly lifted
> then upturned
> spilling joy
>
> on all the spent
> aged greyness
> of the day.

Souster celebrates love as the central experience of inno-
cence, but he has no illusions about it. On King Street the
poet comes across the ugliest woman he has ever seen in
his life. She is with a lover, however, and he looks the
happiest man on the street.

> tonight no doubt he'll climb
> those bulging thighs, board that monstrous stomach,
> he her Columbus, she his fabulous
> new found land.

In most of these poems the poet identifies directly with the
lovers and shares the beauty and joy of their experience.
But this isn't always the case. For Souster is no rebel; he
too belongs to the system. He may not like it but he toler-
ates it and uses it for his own purposes. This makes him in
some sense an outsider (like the businessmen and bankers
and politicians), a stranger, an intruder:

> In another two minutes
> they'd have been at each other
>
> in another minute
> the jeans she was wearing finally down. . . .

> But I, the intruder,
> had to walk in on them,
> I, the stranger, enter
> their kingdom of the woods. . . .

This, for Souster, is an archetypal experience; he returns to it more than once. Souster's most successful poems are in fact poems of middle age, poems in which he can only remember a time of purity, innocence and commitment. "We had that fresh innocence once,/in the summer, by the river, among the willows."

> But tonight it's only
> ghosts I see around these houses,
> the old gang gone,
> every one of them;
> some killed in war,
> some from natural causes,
> the rest, I can guess,
> growing fat and middle-aged
> like me.

Everywhere there is a pervasive sense of guilt. The poet has himself been destroyed by the system and he knows it. He is a stranger and can only remember his days of strength and innocence.

This knowledge breeds sorrow and longing. It also breeds anger. In his most recent poems Souster has been more and more concerned with greed, ugliness and war. Sometimes he handles these themes with the superb skill of an old pro. One of his best-known and most brilliant poems packs more punch in two lines than all the full-page ads published by the International Nickel Company about their operations in Sudbury:

> ". . .But only God can make a tree."
> (He'll never try it in Sudbury.)

The implications are too simple, of course. We are all involved in Sudbury and what it stands for, even the poet. But the couplet is irresistible. Souster gets a laugh too with such a poem as "The Launching":

> Any big event must have
> the Ceremony of the Officials.
>
> I had my officials picked out
> long before starting to build
> my master space rocket.
> They included cabinet ministers,
> arms makers, generals,
> all the boys on the real inside.
>
> When the Big Day came
> they stood on a platform
> at the foot of the monster
> and made speeches
> one after the other.
>
> I let them talk
> as long as they wanted to,
> then, when the last one had finished,
> I pushed back a little door
> in the side of my brain-child
> and invited them to enter.
>
> When the last one had disappeared inside,
> I closed the door, walked very deliberately
> across to the control panel
> and pushed a button.
>
> Imagine my surprise
> when it worked.

This is the familiar Souster mythology, in which cabinet ministers, arms makers and generals, the back-room boys, get the finger. But there is a difference. There is the possibility of resistance. The poet has the last word.

That may be so, but, as Souster knows very well, the back-room boys still control reality. This is the inescapable truth and to Souster it is intolerable. If his tone often becomes strident in the poems of protest it is because he feels himself powerless in the face of ugliness and inhumanity. For Souster as for so many other Canadians his own age and younger, the America of Lyndon Johnson, the America inherited by Richard Nixon, has become the central symbol of oppression.

> America
> only you could create a New York where a new
>   breed of white rats chase slum children
>   through rotting rooms, biting infant flesh
>   with the same relish that some tailor's dummy
>   shows at the same moment downtown taking
>   his first mouthful of ten-dollar steak. . . .

"Death Chant for Mr. Johnson's America" is, in a sense, one of Souster's most important poems. In it he reveals a new energy, a new violence, a new sense of the future.

> America
> your time is running out fast. . . .

We are dealing here not with memories or dreams but with hopes. Souster may not yet have developed the kind of poetic speech he needs to contain his anger. "Death Chant" is not a successful poem, perhaps not a poem at all. But it does indicate new possibilities.

> the real animals, the real monsters
> of this world are never caged or locked up even
>   for a moment,
>
> but are left free to do their killing,

often without the slightest trace of a mark
on a thousand, ten thousand victims,
are called "sir" in clubs, will cause good men to
    jump
     as on a string
when their name is announced, when a telephone
rings.

And these animals live in large houses on quiet
    streets,
have obedient, loving wives who endure every
    pain, every loneliness,
and often, just to show the weakness in the breed,
have at least one untamed, very beautiful
    daughter.

Where will she lead him?

MICHAEL MACKLEM

THE FORTIES

The Hunter

I carry the ground-hog along by the tail
all the way back to the farm, with the blood
dripping from his mouth a couple of drops at a time,
leaving a perfect trail for anyone to follow.

The half-wit hired man is blasting imaginary rabbits
somewhere on our left. We walk through fields steaming
   after rain,
jumping the mud: and watching the swing of your girl's
   hips
ahead of me, the proud way your hand holds the gun,
and remembering how you held it
up to the hog caught in the trap and blew his head in

wonder what fate you have in store for me.

The green temple-dancers of the trees
stretch their fresh unspoiled arms
above the living forests of the grass.

Under a full-rounded moon
frogs blink back green-eyed moons.

Evenings I chose
not to wrestle with maidens there'll be still
the sinewy loins of my thoughts
to press open with the wonder
of a lanced star;

while the green wonderful things
are enemies never forgotten,
snapping shutters over lazy minds, and hiding
too easily the sight and the smell of blood.

The three-pronged print the sandpiper traced
into the sand before we came along,
is as firm, as definite a mark
as any of us will leave
on the hard sand of our world.

In an hour the tide will be in,
and after it's gone the sand will be unmarked
and fresh, only sea's touch on it,
even the tread of the sandpiper
smoothed away by that effortless hand.

It makes me want to laugh
at all the important ones, the polishers
of words and phrases, all the big
little men slaving over the oil:

the print of the sandpiper didn't stay —
which one of you thinks he has fashioned

a finer, more wonderful thing?

They wouldn't understand my haste
in getting out of the rain, in leaving this cold
wind-blowing night for the tavern's
warm heart, for its hot, steaming food,
much beer, and the subtle music
of the violin:
                they seem almost part of the rain
like the policeman in the white cape, white rubber boots
    to the thighs,
who stands in the centre of the traffic
and directs with a sure hand:
                        they seem almost part of the night,
    these two lovers,
with their slow lingering steps, their total unawareness
of everything in this city but their love, the strength,
    the honest lust in their bodies touching
as they walk across the Square. . . .

Not at Angelo's, with wine and spaghetti,
not at the Oak Room, not at Joe's, Mabel's or Tim's Place,
enclosed by no four walls, circled by no chatter, held by no
    unseen hands of music,

but here with the lean cold pushing the light from the stars,
here under ghost buildings, here with silence grown too
    silent,
you and I in this doorway like part of a tomb,
kissing the night with bitter cigaretttes.

With John Sutherland and Louis Dudek

THE FIFTIES

For Irving Layton

In this sweet courtyard of dirt and smells and rot
children play, old men rock in their chairs, and women
hang out the ragged washings of the week. This goes on

winter, summer, fall and spring, year after year,
children playing, old men rocking, women washing,
only it is other children who play, other old men who sit in
    their chairs, other women hanging out clothes.

O this courtyard never changes,
it's still the same dirt, same rot, same smell,
same squirming, crawling tenement, tin-roofed sweat-box
    on the lower slopes of Hell,

open sore on the face of God.

The street is quiet,
the noise through the wall is stilled,
the little cat curled up on the chair,
radio turned off, milk bottles outside the door.

And for now
nothing but sleep and dreams and thoughts of sleep,
not even love keep us awake tonight

as we sink into that strange land
where the blue horses toss
riderless and proud.

The Bourgeois Child

I might have been a slum child,
I might have learned to swear and steal,
I might have learned to drink and whore,

but I was raised a good bourgeois child,
and so it's taken me a little longer.

My grandmother on her bed
struggling for breath,
still sips at life
but would gulp down death.

The Opener

From where I was sitting
it looked like an easy double-play.

But at that precise moment
a sloppy-looking freighter
slipped through the Western Gap
with a clothesline of washing
half the length of her deck,

and the runner going into second
took one look at the ship
and yelled: "Hey, look, they got
my old lady's black pants
flying at the masthead."

And when all the infield
turned around to get a gape,
he made second, stole third,
and scored standing up
the winning run in what otherwise
was one of the cleanest-played openers
in a Toronto ball-park.

Jeannette in a fight
calling in boy friends
to wreck a café,
Jeannette dead drunk
swinging at a cop,
Jeannette on the habit
riding it up
riding it down,
Jeannette in jail
and out again,
Jeannette on the corner
of Dundas and Jarvis
with the old reliable
merchandise for sale.

Some day they'll find her
with a knife in the chest,
or choked to death
by one sheer stocking:

but tonight she's the queen
of this crawling street,
Jeannette with her sweater tight,
proud to show them off
to all the boys:

black hair, big smile,
that's Jeannette.

Red Fruit

From lying there on the bed like a slumbering cat
you turn at my coming like petals opening on a flower;
sinking down to your warmth of face and arms and hands,
I encounter your lips, red fruit I recklessly devour.

Caught in the cone of searchlights over Hamburg
he prayed: Lord, get me out
and I'll make it all up to You. . . .

So next evening
got stoned in the mess, laid a crying
sixteen-year-old up a Darlington lane.

Where once the long valley was
that I rolled down
to the twin towns of your breasts,
to the unpredictable
suburbs of your thighs,

is now a plain
flat and monotonous,
and I don't much like travelling
such usual countryside.

The old lady crushed to death by the Bathurst streetcar
had one cent left in her purse.
                              Which could mean only
one of two things: either she was wary of purse-snatchers
or all her money was gone.
                              If the latter,
she must have known her luck must very soon change
for better or for worse:
                              which this day has decided.

It seems noteworthy to record
that today I saw the ugliest woman
I've ever looked at in my life.

And you might have guessed it —
a man was holding her hand as lovers do,
in fact, looked the happiest one on King Street;

while tonight no doubt he'll climb
those bulging thighs, board that monstrous stomach,
he her Columbus, she his fabulous
new found land.

"Nothing short of scandalous":
words of this highly indignant
highly respectable citizen
on the front page of the daily smear:

young bodies mixed together
in the dark, chasing each other
into the river, and no police
around to stop them.

(What size were your binoculars, pop?)

Just think, old man,
if you were younger
(O a whole lot younger)
you could join in the fun,
chase those lithe maiden flanks
moon-flecked, love-round. . . .

Wouldn't be any fun now, would it?
No hope of catching anything
but a cold up your

you know what, mister.

One of Our Young Soldiers, Drunk,
Spends His First Night in Brussels

The first one was a cow,
he reached up and pulled the bell.
Madame sent up another,
also a cow, he almost
pulled the cord off the wall.
The third was very, very young,
small-breasted, not very tall —
it proved no trouble at all.
He remembered her saying in the night
"You want maybe marry bee-bee?
(hips moving effortlessly)
and he murmuring, "We'll see."

Half-sober in the morning
her beauty seemed a little worn;
then he remembered them kissing
after something she'd done.
He barely made it down the hall.

Outside sunlight mounted a wall.

Set down right in the middle
of old houses waiting their turn
to be torn down but still living
hugely, defiantly;

nestled under the protective arm
of the Russian Orthodox Church
itself lost in this jungle of brick —

the orange-painted shed
seen from a fourth-floor apartment window,

riot of colour among these sombre
clichés of browns, darkened greens and reds,

a burning bush ready
with its revelation.

Kidnapped, beaten,
shot in the head,
his body tied to a ninety-pound weight
and dumped in a river:

a fifteen-year-old schoolboy, negro,
vacationing from Chicago,

enjoying just a sample
of that good old southern
hospitality.

Lowering herself carefully
to avoid being pricked
by more heavenly steeples,

she rested, head full
of birds and grasses,
her Mount Royal pillow;

one arm outstretched
on Jacques Cartier Bridge,
both legs slightly open
at Westmount, St. Louis;

while drawn on a plumb line
from combed-out oval,
St. Lawrence Main.

At night her belly
held a G-string of rubies
down St. Catherine's glitter,
while to keep herself cool
through the fly-blown hours,
her toes dipped themselves
in the sludge of the harbour.

And once she broke wind
and blew the glass
out of three department stores.

This face in the casket, this body
I look at now isn't my friend,
it's all some nightmarish
goof of the newspapers.
                    And I'm sure
any moment now he'll walk in here
puffing on a cigar and say "I can see
I didn't fool you for a minute;
let's get out of here, these places
are depressing as hell. If we hurry
we can still grab a beer at my place
and have enough time to make the ball park
for that single with the Royals."

So I wait and wait
but after five, then ten minutes I know
it's no good.
                    It's you all right, it's you,
hands folded, eyes closed, life drained,
at rest in this blackest of boxes,
somehow terribly, finally you.

O washed-out middle-aged woman
with the swollen legs,
even more grotesque swollen hat,
walking down this afternoon street
on the latest pumps of fashion.

How much would you pay
in good old honest George Washingtons
for that spring-petal sex
of the young negro girl in Macy's
selling slips on the second floor?

How much would you pay
in Lincolns and Madisons
for her black hair of April
her month of May breasts
her pouting June lips
her sweated thighs of mid-July?

The Grey Cup

No doubt it was someone's
idea of a joke —

for on the opening kick-off
when the football spun through the air,

it burst like an over-stuffed balloon,
and floating down in the sun
one great smog of virgin greenbacks. . . .

When order was finally restored
two referees had to be assisted
to the stadium hospital

while at least seven players
lay dying like uprooted turtles
on that striped, bloody field.

The literary life
and the smell of it,

or the young budding author
up assorted rectums.

Better his mother
should have lifted furniture.

THE SIXTIES

A Souster neighbourhood, his home at left

That's the way
we've got to hang on —

like the last patch of snow
clinging to the hillside
crouching at the wood edge
with April done

dirty-white
but defiant

lonely
fighting death.

Boys and ducks (right away
I know I cannot surprise you)
                             boys
wearing rubber boots, skirting the edge
of the frothy river, down which
thirteen ducks back-paddle in the eddies,

suddenly have stones in their hands, their arms arcs
of mischief. The first stones land
much closer than I thought possible (the ducks too)
but they ride out the onslaught, hoping the young arms
will tire of the game (foolish hope of the old!)
finally are forced up as stones rain on them
in an intense whirring of air:
                            go downriver
in a cliché of arrows:
                       leaving boys breathless and happy,
leaving the river valley quiet again, leaving me
half in air with ducks, half with laughing boys.

The Pouring

Porcelain-white
smooth jug
of your body

slowly lifted
then upturned
spilling joy

on all the spent
aged greyness
of the day.

Today at the dawn
for an endless minute
I listened to a bird
fighting for its life
in the claws of a cat,

thinking: much the same way
death will take us all.

Any big event must have
the Ceremony of the Officials.

I had my officials picked out
long before starting to build
my master space rocket.
They included cabinet ministers,
arms makers, generals,
all the boys on the real inside.

When the Big Day came
they stood on a platform
at the foot of the monster
and made speeches
one after the other.

I let them talk
as long as they wanted to,
then, when the last one had finished,
I pushed back a little door
in the side of my brain-child
and invited them to enter.

When the last one had disappeared inside,
I closed the door, walked very deliberately
across to the control panel
and pushed a button.

Imagine my surprise
when it worked.

"Too many churches, not enough bawdy houses,"
this frank young Englishman
fresh from the London flesh-pots
wrote to a friend after spending
his first week in Toronto (1885).

But later that year
was seduced in his own room
by the daughter of an Anglican minister,
and the next spring opened up the first
all-night mission ever seen on Yonge Street.

On the Way to the Store

She stops on the sidewalk
because some of the bottles
have worked loose and fallen
from her bundle-buggy.

It's hard to bend down,
she's not young any more.
I know that she curses
fumbling with shaky hands,
and I'd help if I could,

but I'm on a street-car
going swiftly by, can't do
a single thing for her,
can only hope she gets
to the beer-store and back
without one cracked bottle.

That's about all the luck
I can safely wish her.

I sit down to write a poem about you,
but my good right hand keeps getting up from the desk
and running across the hall to the bedroom
where you're sleeping,
                          to return in a minute
first with your right breast, then with your left,
then we try once again, and again. . . .

So, as you may have guessed, your poem
never does get written.

The Extra Blanket

Somewhere in the night
I wake up shivering
from cold
      and reach out
pull something over me
that is warm and breathes
has lips a nose
soft hair and arms
and crevices and other
wild wonderful compartments

reason to spare
why winter's never cold
or long enough.

Three o'clock
school's out.

Only time of day
the dead really hate,
as the children take
the short-cut through the park
and sliding over
the flat-lying tombstones
run on and out
and away

taking their warmth
their laughter
back to the living.

Good to be back
in the old house. To hear the toilet's
sudden boil and simmer-down. To walk
along the upstairs hall and know
where the floor will creak and not creak:

to find the same cobweb
crouched in that same secret corner,
to feel faithful bed-springs
warm to their work again!

Push your buds, lilac,
as a young girl feels
her nipples shiver
then suddenly harden
as her lover fondles her

as the spring wind tonight
takes you in every branch.

I watch,
the beggar with the one leg
hand holding a pencil
watches

the woman stopped with her back to us
fumbling in her purse for either
a dime for that pencil or a subway token

my eyes
the eyes of this ragged man
say together:
nothing else in the whole world at this moment
is of more importance.

Thrush

The thrush on the farthest-out bough
sings the best song his heart will allow.

And if we haven't liked what we've heard
there's tomorrow and another bird.

Easter Sunday

The day begins
too well. The wind
summer's, out
of season,
the sun, shy
behind clouds,
surely will burst through
in brilliance
soon.

But rain with thunder
before evening.
Behind the stone
rolled away
another and another
without end.

Abandon of cats
making love in the cold

enough to send shivers
through our warm, lazy bed!

The first real year
I pitched baseball
we played straight across
from the roundhouse,

and every time
I got jammed up
in a three-and-two count,
I stalled around
till a black screen of smoke
blew across, then wound up
and threw it up the gut
with no worries at all. . . .

But like everything else
that was too good to last—
the next year they tore
the old roundhouse down,
and I only finished seven
out of thirteen starts,

the smoke gone forever
you might say
from my fast one.

All animals like me
now get themselves out of the cold
into some kind of lair
cavernous or small,
to curl up more like a ball
than anything else and sleep
an untroubled sleep of snow,
which sifting down endlessly white
and curdled thick as cream
makes the four-poster of a dream.

Just about everything
or everyone
has passed up or down:

William Lyon Mackenzie's boys
on the quick way down
from Montgomery's Tavern,
Year of Tyrants
1837.

Wendell Willkie smiling
his 1940 smile
with planes overhead
and the crowds gone crazy,
the year he could have made
Prime Minister!

But until today
never elephants.
Ten grey eminences moving
with the daintiest of steps
and the greatest unconcern
up the canyon.
                Too bored to yawn
or toss the fools riding them,
they slowly twist their trunks
and empty their bowels
at a pace that keeps
the two men following
with shovels and hand-cart
almost swearingly busy.

"Mr. Hill" my mother calls it,
not needing another name
though being a plant
it must have one.
                    Named
for a friend of her family
who brought it to their garden,
one spring night, 1919.
                              And that week-end
was drowned in a canoe
up north.

Kept by my mother
all these years, and tended
with the greatest love.
Then, to preserve the legacy,
one part of it planted
in this garden.
                    Where it fights
its battle with cutworms,
green, tattered leaves
spread in summer to the sun.

Fights so well, my darling,
it's not hard to believe
it may outlive us all.

I don't care
how high the clouds are,
how white they curdle
in the whey of the sky,
or if the sun
is kind to the flowers,
or why the wind
plays at storms in the trees.

The robin hiding
in the garden bushes
has a broken wing.

Death must come hard
to these old farms waiting
the weeds to cover them.
Houses rot in the sun
till doors slip their hinges,
windows sag, and hole-up
their shame with much spider-smoke,
barns rot in the rain,
roofs bare plucked skeletons,
with weathervane winds
always in on the kill.

But these farms wait with dignity
for the thistle to climb,
the goldenrod thicken,
for that final falling
and touch-to with earth:
then sleep with always
some warm star above.

Church Bells, Montreal

Against the hard
clear ring of the bells

measure that quick
whispered tick of our lives.

Columbus Grads Baseball Club, 1940

Vitore, Bugala, Moszyniski, where are you now?
Angelis, Croswell, Calgone, what has time done with you?

You wouldn't remember me, the kid brought up
for a taste of senior ball. But I remember
all of you, after twenty years and more,
just like yesterday. . . .

Was it down at Belleville I had my first under-age beer,
sitting in the men's room, glass in front of me, liking
the taste of it so I didn't have to pretend?
                                        Was it up
at Eglinton Park they called us "dirty Wops," and baseball
   bats went swinging
at more than just fastballs?
                        What night did we walk in our
   spikes
all the way from Stanley Park to the Pits by the back lanes?

That was our last year of baseball: the War waited for us.
No more dusty hours on the diamond, the hand-throbbing
   sting of the bat
stroking line-drives, no more third strikes with a round-
   house curve.
The War waited for us, to take us, to grind us,
at the end of that season!
                        O Krycia, Wagman, McDowell,
heroes of my youth,
                  where are you now?
                              And where am I?

Street of my boyhood
(I lived right around the corner),
quiet, leaf-heavy street
of West Toronto.
                        Here,
behind that house, in the lane,
from garage roofs we ambushed
the Nelles Street gang,
pinned them down with catapults,
then, out of acorns,
forgot all our strategy
and ran like hell.
                        Out this door
on Christmas Day
of all days, that queer girl
came sleep-walking, nightgown and all,
and even the snow underfoot
couldn't waken her.
                        At this number lived
the grease-monkey boys,
(their Stutz Touring shined
to a blinding dazzle),
who sometimes took me
as heart-pounding passenger
out the Queen Elizabeth,
to run her, gun her
past eighty on a straight stretch,
with the extra spice
of maybe a speed-cop
coming out of nowhere.
                        On this lawn
I pounded and bloodied
my next-to-worst enemy,
and curiously found
it wasn't fun anymore. . . .

But tonight it's only
ghosts I see around these houses,
the old gang gone,
every one of them;
some killed in war,
some from natural causes,
the rest, I can guess,
growing fat and middle-aged
like me.
      But not one of them
comes back here, I know,
they've got better sense:

just the crazy poet
well hooked on the past,
a sucker for memories.

Paper handkerchief
or silk

it's how you wave
that puts the kiss
in goodbye.

I can almost see
my father's canoe
pointing in from the lake,
him paddling,
mother hidden
in a hat of fifty years ago.

Turning now up a stream
clear-flowing through marsh
(not mud-brown like today):

gliding under the same
railway bridge we cross under,
slipping by the same giant
stepping-stones of rock
standing up so like ramparts:

moving on to those quieter
summer-singing reaches,
the calling of birds
making speech difficult.

Lost finally, perhaps forever,
behind ferns swallowing banks,
bent trees overarching sky,

drifting the summer
labyrinths of love.

Unadulterated poetry
starts to happen at King and Bay
as the four ditch-diggers
slowly converge on the sparrow
who's lost all power
in his wings but a last desperate
flutter that doesn't keep him
long away from the hairy
meat-hook of a hand
which, cupped, for a moment
is his prison —
                  but now becomes (the miracle!)
warm-beating soft cell of skin
whose other name is love.

The Bud

All that flowering's nothing,
really nothing to me —

it's the about-
to-break look of the bud,
promise of sudden
burst-out from the dark
into light
into sunshine dazzling.

And you wonder:
could a life too
be as suddenly reborn?

The Worm

Don't ask me how he managed
to corkscrew his way
through the King Street pavement,
I'll leave that to you.

All I know is
there he was,
circling, uncoiling
his shining three inches,
wiggling all ten toes
as the warm rain fell
in that dark morning street
of early April.

When summer returns, these same willows will come **alive**,
burst bud and throw
a green band along
the mud banks of the river.

When I was a kid, nine or ten years old,
we played our games of cowboys and Indians
among them. More than once surprised
young couples in those thickets,
who, thinking themselves well hidden,
had abandoned themselves to their loving.

I think we were more
surprised and embarrassed than **they were**,
for they said nothing to us, made no move
to leave off their pleasure,
while we retreated, confused,
not old or bold enough to know
our easy advantage.

Was it later we collected
soiled sheaths of their mating, spearing them
on the points of sticks?

It may have been.
We had that fresh innocence once,
in the summer, by the river, among the willows.

Bill

All day I've tried
to recall your face,
this through the time-block
of twenty years and more. . . .

And this evening it comes —
now I know
that after 16 1/2 kills
(and no better for it),
the DSO, DFC and bar,

the biggest
brawliest
(curly-headed) kid
in our high school

went for his.

A thick mucous film
now covered the eyeball.

Out it comes or she'll die
the vet warned us.

Better have her destroyed
someone else said.

Today she lives on
in our house,
number one
one-eyed cat.

No trouble at all
with the good right eye
of our love.

Jewels

Who says
nothing beautiful ever happens
in Toronto?

Just think of this —

Bobby Hackett coming suddenly
out of Whaley, Royce on Yonge Street,
holding in his hand a gleaming trumpet
which catching the late rays
of the afternoon sun makes jewels,
crown jewels flashing in my mind long after
he's waved for a taxi, driven south
into the soft auto haze. . . .

Death Chant for Mr. Johnson's America

America
you seem to be dying
America
moving across the forty-ninth parallel each day a stronger
more death-laden stench; wafting inshore from off the
Great Lakes the same unmistakable stink, so unlike
the usual putrefaction of these waters
America
the cracks are beginning to show
America
I knew you were marching to doom the night a young
American told me: "There at Buffalo I saw our flag
flying, then fifty yards further on your Maple Leaf, and
I thought: thank God I'll never have to cross that line
going back again."
America
even your best friends of yesterday are now proud to be
your enemies
America
that time is past when the sight of the Stars and Stripes
flying at the masthead of your ships can calm the
"natives," that time too is over when a detachment of
Marines on landing can still restore law and order and
a continuance of the prescribed vested interests
America
there will be no more San Juan Hills, no more Remember
the Maines, no more sad empires of United Fruit
America
your time is running out fast
America
you haven't changed at all since you sent your New York
State farm boys across the Niagara to conquer us once
and for all, since you printed your handbills promising
French Canadians sweet liberation from their oppres-

sors, since you looked the other way as Fenians played
toy soldier across our borders
America
you're sitting on your own rumbling volcano
America
only you could create a New York where a new breed of
white rats chase slum children through rotting rooms,
biting infant flesh with the same relish that some
tailor's dummy shows at the same moment downtown
taking his first mouthful of ten-dollar steak while
beaming across at his equally overdressed partner as
she too presses her teeth into the meat course, only
you could create squads of drunks lying in doorways,
addicts readying fixes in dirty washroom heavens, only
you could build these terrifying buildings reaching
up through dirt noise and smog-death for a breath of
clean air somewhere at the thousand-foot level, only
you could fashion East River mountains of used cars,
graveyards of King Auto more mysterious than ele-
phant burial grounds, only you could spawn the greed
and corruption of a Wall Street with its ticker-tape
fortune-cookie dreams, its short-sell nightmares, only
you could conceive this monster and only you will be
the one to destroy it pier by pier, block by block,
citizen by citizen
America
you seem bent on self-destruction
America
today you are Ginsberg's nightmare brought up-to-date,
today you would sicken Hart Crane, make him puke
on his Brooklyn Bridge, today you are fast becoming
Jeffers' perishing republic all set to vanish in one final
blast with the rest of a despairing world
America
you seem bent on taking that world along with you just for
the ride

America

phoney as a Hollywood cowboy mainstreet, laughable as
Rockefeller with his ten-cent pieces, vulgar as a Las
Vegas nightclub, brave as your airmen machine-
gunning river-front refugees in broad daylight of
Dresden's holocaust

America

you have learned from everyone's history but your own

America

all the Kennedys left cannot help you now

America

I've learned how you operate, I know how votes are man-
aged, who has his coat pockets stuffed with bribes,
who finds himself asked to be Assistant Secretary of
this or that, who is tossed out finally with nothing left
but bitterness eating at his heart

America

you kept Pound locked up all those years — he had you
pegged, Usura, he had you dead to rights, betrayers
of Jefferson, he had you figured out good so you left
him caged and cooking in the sun at Pisa hoping to
drive him mad — but he put the record straight about
Roosevelt; you hoped to bury him but instead he
walks a free man now, his vision haunting you with its
signature of doom

America

was promises nobody has kept or ever intended keeping

America

how do you turn quiet home-loving men in five short years
into hate-fired Black Muslim avengers who write,
scream out to their brothers: break doors, smash
windows at night or anytime, bust in every store
window, drag out all you can carry, set fire, kill or
maim Whitey, pump holes in every dirty cop or get
him good with a brick or your own two hands

America

give it all back to the Indians if they can stand the smell
   and the flies around the corpse
America
how easily your myths tarnish, how expendible are your
   heroes, how quickly, how easily you swallow good
   people into your patented garbage disposal, grinding
   them down into nice little pieces to be carted away to
   the dump with the same care accorded the ashes of
   dead Japanese soldiers (but none the less garbage,
   waste products of your restless unsatisfied ambition
   hanging like a cancer cloud, a plague of slowly
   spreading death over the world)
America
you have been tested and found wanting
America
the world has watched you in Vietnam and even its hard-
   ened stomach has been turned, you have all but
   buried yourself in your own Coca-Cola beer-can
   litter, your bar-to-bar Saigon filth so well aped by the
   small men you came to save but instead have cor-
   rupted forever; after your crazy "weed killer" squad-
   rons have bared all the trees, after your Incinderjell
   has roasted all available corpses, then perhaps we'll
   see at last every barbed-wire death camp, count every
   tin-can house left standing, see how much rice still
   grows — after the last plane has been shot down out of
   the sky we'll be able to see who still owns all the graft
   concessions, who hands out the government payoffs
   and opens unnumbered bank accounts in Switzerland
   daily — but until then we watch as your Marines ad-
   vance, as the underground bunkers are cooked out one
   by one, as the aircraft let go their terror bombs hoping
   these latest villages have a few more VC than the
   ones raided yesterday — the whole world watches,
   wonders how it will end, while you twine yourself
   more and more with the dragon coils of your own pre-

meditated meddling
America
there is really nothing left to do but die with a certain
gracefulness
really nothing left to do
America
in the name of God you never trusted, e pluribus unum

February, 1968

EPILOGUE

America
tonight fiery candles of the black man's mass burn crimson
in the skies of Washington, Chicago, tributes from the
ghettos to your Gandhi struck down by bullets of hate,
the Gun used again to work out history, the Gun in the
hands of the lawless once again making jungles of your
streets, mockery of your laws, the Gun that gave you
birth, that burned on its red-hot gun-barrel flesh of
brother turned against brother, once again supreme —
so bring out machine-guns, unsling the shot-guns, line
up the sights from the armoured car, shoot to kill,
shoot to kill, shoot to kill, kill, kill, kill
America

April 5, 1968

In this room nothing
but dark and our breathing.

We swim we drown
in the depths of our loving.

I god of this life
the mad world's master,

you warm sun circling
my earth of amazement.

In another two minutes
they'd have been at each other

in another minute
the jeans she was wearing finally down. . . .

But I, the intruder,
had to walk in on them,

I, the stranger, enter
their kingdom of the woods,

catch them with the lazy look
of loving glazed in their eyes —

then as I crashed away
down the path, their laughter
mocking, yet tender,
followed me, biting
at the tips of my heels.

The Underpass

Under can be
such a mad
echo way
of going through.

In the TV studio the poet
has begun to read his poem
"The Pomegranates,"
a good one, he hasn't written
too many better.
                    But someone
has placed four real (live?) pomegranates
in a bowl, and beside it another bowl
in which two more of the fruit
have been halved and quartered,
the whole thing sitting on a table now
with spotlights and cameras
on it.
       Strange how the eyes
cut off the words my ears strain to hear,
eyes pulling me away
from the poem and the poet,
all because of this radiant, natural fact.

Is it because we are tired
of too many words, even good ones,
or have we let the eyes
overpower the mind, leaving eyes
too undisciplined?
                    While I ponder this
and a poet exclaims on about pomegranates,
the whole barn of a building glows
from those fruited halves, those quarters,
blood-red on a table. . . .

Someone's always late for every meeting,
especially poetry readings —

                        tonight it's a moth
swept in on spring air through the open window
right in the middle of Dennis Lee reading
his third Civil Elegy:

                  flutters once across the room
so surely, so gaily it takes
all my breath away.

               Then as suddenly becomes
some part of this room, like a spot on the wall,
or sits down underneath a chair — or is my imagination
working overtime? — changes in the wink of an eye
to the young unspoiled face
of a girl in the third row smiling up at me.

Lady or Mister Squirrel
who slipped, slithered down
our disused chimney
last week or the week before,

makes clawing, scratching
noises tonight, and I stand
on a chair and scratch, claw back
a little in return.

But I haven't the urgency
in my signalling that something
trapped in a dark hole and starving
to death must have, couldn't
have it.
       For me it's a game
for a few minutes, then I'll think
of something else to pass the time
and move on.
           No way
for him or her
to get through at me (I tell myself),
and the wall's too thick
to let any hint of the slow smell
of dying come in.

I scratch back again.

Standing in the dead bee-keeper's orchard, morning heat of the day not great yet, bending over, picking up windfalls till I have a handful, then straightening up to throw apple after apple in my best Columbus Boys' Baseball Club style at the gaping hole in the barn's side.

Barn that's hard by the house and collapsing slowly, barn filled high with hay that rots in the dusty silence, barn dying much like this house and the great barn beyond now nothing more than a few scattered timbers the wreckers couldn't use.

Wonder what he'd say, that bee-keeper, seeing me pitching apples till my right arm aches, bound to get three in a row through the hole or let my arm fall from its socket, stubborn myself as that man to have my way, not counting the cost.

Maybe he'd think me stung silly by his bees, turned a little mad (only his bees went this spring, sold to the highest bidder); maybe he'd just lean back on the rickety snake fence, watching the city boy work out his madness, watching the green apples streak toward the barn's side, splattering mostly against the dry wood, pulp of them formed in a pattern of uselessness, juice of them trickling down in a frivolous wasting.

My battered Christ
of Yonge Street
now suddenly old,
more unwashed
more ragged than ever,

shaking so badly
you have to look twice
at the postcard
he holds out
to decide it's the same one
he couldn't sell
all last week.

Pact

Soon, all too soon
winter will storm in
fall heavily on us.

So this very morning
my gnarled, so-bent-over
crab-apple tree
and I have made
a very solemn pact.

Until its last
red fruit has fallen
we are not defeated,
and will concede nothing.

High priest of summer,
with you in your temple
at noon-blaze the world
goes suddenly mad
with the first frenzied wail
of your pipes, crazy-mad,
uncontrolled — and we shriek
in our heads with you
as the sound goes higher
higher, higher,
                    then break
at the climax, part slowly
on the bed — writhing over,
nerve ends spent —
waiting in the hot
naked room for your cry
to begin again,
to mock us or anyone
mad enough to ape
or play at your madness
with a little of our own.

Shoe Store

A good thirty years since I stood in this store,
shy boy of fifteen become forty-five.
Nothing's changed much, except the front
is a shoe store complete with fancy mirrors,
theatre folding seats, usual boxes piled
rack after rack to the ceiling.

The shoe repair's well to the rear,
separately walled off: in the old days
it was all shoe-making — whirling belts,
gleaming stitchers.
                    One thing that hasn't changed
is the shoemaker, no more bald
than he was then, stooped a little more
in the shoulders perhaps as he bends
over a buffer, working a pair of pumps
back and forth with complete absorption,
all the long years of skill centred
at the ends of his fingers, while I stand here quietly
(not wanting to break the spell I've somehow started)
for minutes before he notices me and nods.

Polish immigrant before the War, hardly able
to mouth an English word, he felt alien and lost
among us. All the strength in his body,
all his cunning, put to the service of his child,
beautiful girl I can scarcely remember,
early a piano virtuoso.
                        Well, he's prospered,
no longer lives above the store. I wonder
if his wife's still alive, if all goes well
with his daughter.

But he wouldn't remember me,
so why bother? Why not leave it all
mercifully unknown?
                    I ask him simply,
"Can you stitch this up for tomorrow?"
and he answers, "Sure."
                        I don't ask for a ticket
and he doesn't offer one. I walk out slowly
between his mirrors, his shoe boxes,
close the door on thirty years gone forever.

The RAF called it
The Dresden Special. . . .

One hundred thirty thousand
charred bodies jammed together
between two bread slices.

But even at that
jolly old Sir Winston
had no trouble lifting it
in his pudgy fingers.

After a bite or two
he smacked his lips, grunting,
Just the way I like Nazis,
very well done. . . .

". . .But only God can make a tree."
(He'll never try it in Sudbury.)

Ducks, Five O'Clock, Late November

Last slant of the day's
sun lightening the murk brown
of river water.

On which ducks land
with a ripple-drip
of webbed feet
trailing. On which
the same ducks
upturn into the same
brown water
ice-cold enough to make
my teeth chatter
watching them.
               Or so
to feed
each delicious shiver
I imagine it.

"Between sets one night
I noticed I was spitting blood
for the first time ever.

I was blowing great
and didn't want to quit,
so I had three quick doubles
to fix things over.

That fixed them *good.*
I passed out on the stand.

At the hospital
they couldn't pierce a vein,
had to drill a hole
in one leg to get
a transfusion going.

For a week I rocked back
between life and death,
not caring,
without any pain.

Then one morning
opened my eyes
and right away
found myself casing
the nurses going by.

From then on I knew
I had a few choruses
still left to blow. . . ."

And keep blowing them
like you are tonight
till hell cools out, Bill!

For Jim Lowell

Luke Hamlin's down there warming up, his baseball cap as battered as ever, not looking one day older than he did in the Forties and early Fifties, still with plenty of stuff left, his change-up floating in there slowly enough to count every stitch on the ball, his fast one when it comes digging with a smack in the catcher's mitt, his curve a butterfly that can't make up its mind until the very last the direction it really wants to take.

And Rocky's out there too, Rocky Nelson's down on one knee in the on-deck circle, working his plug tobacco softer while his two big meat-hooks of hands softly grip three bats, two of which he'll throw toward the bat boy just before taking his slow purposeful walk to the batter's box. He also doesn't look any older than he did in those years he led the League in home runs and runs batted in, besides making put-outs at first look like duck soup, nothing at all.

Now Luke's through his warm-up, saunters out toward the mound. The catcher moves in behind home plate, in a moment will take the last few pitches before the game gets under way. Rocky's up on his feet now, swings his three bats and tosses two away, the ritual of discarding the lumber, then shuffles up to the plate, ready for business.

It's a warm summer afternoon here at Maple Leaf Stadium, a Saturday in late June, to be exact. There's a light breeze blowing in off the lake but not enough to bother the players, the sun far enough around so it doesn't shine directly in a batter's eyes. Right about now the umpire should be yelling "Play ball" and moving back behind the catcher to get set for the first pitch of the game. At this moment the ten to twelve thousand fans in the stands should be breaking out into a minor roar as the batter stands in there swinging his bat, waiting for the delivery. But today there's no umpire dressed in black behind the plate or out behind first or second, and certainly no crowd in the stands — for the stands are gone, the seats, the climbing lettered aisles, and most noticeably the overhanging roof shadowing it all — there's nothing up there where the smell of hot dogs used to float around, where peanuts were cracked, where ice-cold pop was guzzled deliciously; there's nothing up there but a mass of rusted iron girders, naked arms pointing uselessly at the sky. The wreckers have done their job very well indeed.

But strangely enough the right-field fence still remains and Rocky Nelson as he steps to the plate gives it one quick glance and takes his place in the batter's box. Luke Hamlin's ready too, he gives his battered cap one last touch and toes the rubber. Then he kicks and throws a fast one on the outside to the left-handed batter which Rocky only watches streak by. A beautiful strike and you wonder why Rocky wasn't ready for that one, didn't paste it good. But Rocky only shifts his chaw to the other side of his cheek, wiggles his body a little, his feet still in that half-turned-away stance that has puzzled baseball writers for years but works very well indeed for him, and looks out again at Luke. Luke has finished tugging on his trouser belt, touches his cap and steps on the rubber again. He goes into his wind-up.

And the pitch? Surely not another fast one — Luke must know Rocky will be ready for that move. A change-up? The logical time to throw it, which is probably why he won't. Well then, a good, sharp-breaking curve cutting in close on the left-hand batter?

That's what it is, breaking beautifully with a last second twitch to it. But Rocky's spotted the pitch early and his bat comes around, a lightning parallel arc to his body. The clean sharp crack of swinging wood, real wood, meeting a baseball head-on, is what we hear.

And there it goes, folks, bang down the right-field line but just now curving a shade inside, still rising as it reaches the outfield grass, up, up, there it goes, folks, a home run over the right-field fence with twenty feet or more to spare, still it goes on rising, rising, over ghosts of Little Norway, over the marina and a hundred pleasure craft at dockside, still rising it moves out over the bay, heading for the Island, lost now among all that green of water, blue of sky. . . .

And now we look around us, forced to realize at last that we are all alone in this great empty field of weed-high grass, only the iron girders of the gone-forever grandstand pointing up almost despairingly in the afternoon sunshine, no crowd or crowd-roar, only the endless traffic going by on Fleet Street — and we know now we're witnessing one more little death among so many dyings — life will go on, still beautiful and strange, but never in quite the same way as yet another boyhood fantasy goes under: after today not even the poet's wildest imaginings can make that world of baseball come alive again, brave shining world of clean uniforms, of graceful strategic manoeuvres; it's all gone, there's nothing left to do now but go on home, gracefully, if possible, this time without even as much as a bright-coloured rain-check in the pocket, which found months later in kinder days still promised baseball in another year. . . .

July, 1968

I haven't seen you on the main floor
for a month, she tells me,
they seem to keep you animals
well caged down there.
We both smile at her joke (an old one),
knowing the real animals, the real monsters
of this world are never caged or locked up even for a
    moment,

but are left free to do their killing,
often without the slightest trace of a mark
on a thousand, ten thousand victims,
are called "sir" in clubs, will cause good men to jump as on
    a string
when their name is announced, when a telephone rings.

And these animals live in large houses on quiet streets,
have obedient, loving wives who endure every pain, every
    loneliness,
and often, just to show the weakness in the breed,
have at least one untamed, very beautiful daughter.

THE SEVENTIES

Queen Anne's Lace

It's a kind of flower
that if you didn't know it
you'd pass by the rest of your life.

But once it's pointed out
you'll look for it always,
even in places
where you know it can't possibly be.

You will never tire
of bending over to examine,
to marvel at this,
the shyest filigree of wonder
born among grasses.

You will imagine poems
as brief, as spare,
so natural with themselves
as to take breath away.

The spider outside our window
had a problem. A chunk of rose petal
in falling had grabbed hold
of his net and stayed there,
somehow content.

What to do? Charlie didn't like
the taste of it, the thing took up
far too much trapping area,
and yet gave the place a little class
sadly lacking before, so he dallied,
not moving it.
                    Then one day, inspiration!
He painted up a sign in bug's blood,
hung it out proudly:

HAPPY CHARLIE'S ROSE GARDENS
WHERE YOU'LL ALWAYS MEET A FRIEND

The End of Summer

Frenzied whine
of cicada's bandsaw
is silent now.

Only wood uncut
that branch he's fastened to.

Pictures from a Long-Lost World: 1912

The young officers of cavalry
fresh from Sofia sit stiff-backed on horses
as they shout across the now-silent battlefield.

It has been a most glorious victory.
Another Turkish fort captured
with a loss of only fifty soldiers.

Dead comrades lie at their horses' feet.
They lie singly or piled together.
If there is time they'll be buried,
if not buzzards will strip them clean.

In this year of rapid advances
nothing is certain.

Still grabbing
at that golden ring?

The ride's the thing.

Flies clinging
to a tablecloth
even with the last crumb
gone

Such young
age-whitened faces

waiting
through the hours

for food
dope
money

love

To look at the world
and all things in it

as wide-eyed
amazed
full of wonder

as Max
my fur-ball
my endless tail

cat of pure joy!

The Gift

To see his delight
to be given a newly-
cut handful of flowers,

to watch how he holds them
tightly yet tenderly
as he walks across the Square.

Old wizened-up Chinaman
you have made this morning for me:

from now on all flowers
will be carried this way!

He smiling eager
curly-headed Adam

She dark-haired
temptress Eve

tongue and ear
kissing
on the subway platform
(what's coming next?)

Nobody's told them
subways are for sleeping.

A hundred eyes on them
but they only laugh
in their aloneness

at the loveless.

Perhaps because he doesn't know he's being watched, this stacker of bodies goes about his business naturally, relaxed, not with the military stiffness he'd adopt, say, if the Inspector-General were in the vicinity.

This morning he's being kept fairly busy, the stretcher bearers bringing in one corpse after another, which they dump casually on the ground, then go away to make another pickup. It's his job, then, to lift the dead bodies up so they form a neat pile on the large flat carts made especially for the purpose. He's a large, heavy man, seems to handle the bodies quite easily. As he picks one up he turns the body so that it rests face down on the pile. Sometimes he doesn't get one placed exactly right, the head sticking out several inches beyond the others; and being the perfectionist he is he'll tug or push that particular body to get it back into line — once he even gives a kick when his hands don't seem to be making the right progress. He's a sensitive man, too, even with day after day of this bloody work, and where a neck shows without a head he'll cover it with a piece of burlap standing by for just such a purpose.

Then, when he can no longer lift more bodies onto the pile, he finishes the layer he's working on and begins another fresh stack. It's hard work and he's beginning to feel his age. He'll be glad when the new helper the sergeant has promised him arrives. He hopes he'll be an older man like himself — the young nowadays don't seem to take any pride in a job well done. Why, if the dead could see themselves lying here they'd be struck by the soldierly neatness of things, all ends properly in place, everything done with precision and despatch as on the most exacting of parade-squares!

Copyright © 1972 by Raymond Souster

"The Hunter," "Print of the Sandpiper," "Dominion Square,"
"Night Watch," "City Hall Street," "Where the Blue Horses,"
"The Bourgeois Child," "My Grandmother," "The Opener,"
"World Traveller at Twenty-One," "The New Mattress," "Death
by Streetcar," "The Orange-Painted Shed," "Welcome to the
South," "Like the Last Patch of Snow," "Boys and Ducks," "The
Extra Blanket," "Loyalist Burial Ground, Saint John," "Home-
coming," "Lilac Bush in Spring," "Decision on King Street,"
"Thrush" and "Easter Sunday" are reprinted from *The Colour
of the Times*; "Jeannette," "Abandon of Cats," "All Animals
Like Me," "Ten Elephants on Yonge Street," " 'Mr. Hill,' "
"Broken Day," "Old Farms, Bruce Peninsula," "Church Bells,
Montreal," "Looking at Old Photographs" and "Armadale
Avenue Revisited" from *Ten Elephants on Yonge Street*, all by
permission of McGraw-Hill Company of Canada. "The Pouring"
and "The Roundhouse" are reprinted from *Lost & Found* by
permission of Clarke, Irwin & Company.
Library of Congress Catalogue Card No. 72-77040
ISBN 0 88750 052 8 (hardcover)
ISBN 0 88750 053 6 (softcover)
Back jacket photograph by Henry Fox. Book design by Michael
Macklem. Printed in Canada by The Coach House Press
PUBLISHED IN CANADA BY OBERON PRESS